D0524235

*A sampling
of the sound advice
you can expect
from this invaluable book:*

If you should recklessly decide to give your cat a bath, change your mind and don't. If you still insist on being hardheaded about the whole affair, get some soap designed to do the job, draw a tub of water brought carefully up to cat-body temperature, and line up a towel or two, iodine, sutures, gauze—a bottle of brandy wouldn't be amiss, either—and a pair of chain-mail gauntlets. You might also notify your next of kin, if you are the type that really plans ahead. . . .

How to Live with a Calculating Cat

by Eric Gurney

PUBLISHED BY POCKET BOOKS NEW YORK

Acknowledgment to
William Nettleton
for his text

POCKET BOOKS, a Simon & Schuster division of
GULF & WESTERN CORPORATION
1230 Avenue of the Americas, New York, N.Y. 10020

Copyright © 1962 by Prentice-Hall, Inc.

Published by arrangement with Prentice-Hall, Inc.

All rights reserved, including the right to reproduce this book
or portions thereof in any form whatsoever.
For information address Prentice-Hall, Inc.,
Englewood Cliffs, N.J. 07632

ISBN: 0-671-41693-6

First Pocket Books printing November, 1976

12   11   10   9   8

POCKET and colophon are trademarks of Simon & Schuster.

Printed in the U.S.A.

Dedicated to my wife,

NANCY,

whose help, advice,
and love for cats
made this book possible

Contents

How to Live

with

a Calculating

Cat

1

The Calculating
Cat in History

Webster defines a cat as a carnivorous mammal long domesticated and kept by man as a pet or for catching rats and mice.

An early experiment in friendship ends in dismal
failure for man.

Man-Eating Uncle Tiger and Little Nephew.

Having a cat is quite simple today. But it was not always so. It may be assumed that these first attempts to domesticate the cat, though entirely satisfactory from the cat's point of view, were not completely successful from man's. Therefore, it is only fitting that we pay a silent moment of tribute to those brave men and women of the past.

Yes, prehistoric man had to learn a lot about cats, and the first thing he found out was that there were a good many different kinds of cats . . . mostly the wrong kind.

Cousin Bob (lynx canadensis), a very careful and cautious relative.

Great Grandpappy Sabre Tooth and Well-Adjusted House Cat.

Chock full of courage, Cousin Jaguar meets
a distant relation.

His Majesty, Uncle Lion, the King
of the Jungle, and his Better Half.

Cousin Cheetah, known as "Speedy" for short.

His experience with lions was not much better than with those horrid sabre-tooth tigers. And the leopard was forever sneaking up on him from behind. The wildcat lived up to his name; and the polecat, though inadvertently leading man to the discovery of perfume, had a trick with his tail that was disastrous. In fact, it got to the point where man was ready to call the whole business off, when out of the forest came this little creature:

Man froze and waited to see what would happen. The claws of this seemingly friendly creature remained hidden, and nothing happened when the little critter slowly waved his tail to and fro. Tentatively, man reached over and petted this non-odiferous, non-wild, non-man-eating creature. The cat purred. Snuggled. He fitted Webster's definition of a cat to a T.

The cat surveyed his new home and promptly drove all the rats and mice out of the cave. Once he had finished with them, he started on the food supply. This prompted man to move all his things to a higher watermark, and may have led to the development of the table, which has come to be a bone of contention between cat and man ever since.

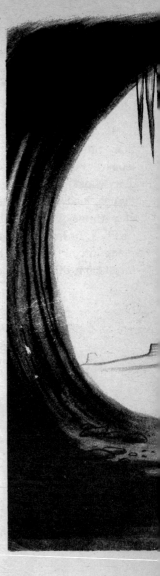

It took years to learn how to spell cat.

The first we read about cats is on ancient tablets written in Sanskrit. It is not known who first wrote about cats. The author forgot to chip out his name on the bottom.

The Egyptians wrote extensively about cats, and in the time of the Pharoahs, cats were pretty much in control of things. They were treasured for their beauty and their usefulness. Women adopted their graces, as smart women have done ever since. They copied the shape and style of the cat's eyes in their makeup. And they adopted that mysterious and aloof manner which had attracted man to cats in the first place—probably in hope that it would do the same thing for them. Cleopatra found this experiment entirely satisfactory, which didn't do Mark Antony much good.

20

"Copy Cat" comes from the ancient Egyptian.

Then, as now, the cat had an economic value too. Egypt was the great granary of the civilized world. However, their towering warehouses could be seen by every rat and mouse for miles. They took the first road to the granaries they could find. The result would have been the thinning of the human population and the fattening of the rodent one, except for the cat. He stopped this invasion dead in its tracks. The priests who were in charge of the granaries decided to reward the cat for his fine performance. But they did not want to give him anything in the way of tangible assets, so they took the cheap way out. They made the cat a god. In those days

21

this was about the equivalent of being made an assistant vice-president of something. Also they made it a crime punishable by death to take a cat out of Egypt.

The Egyptians called the cat *felis caffre,* and we may laugh at them for making this small animal a god, but our own ancestors called him *felis cattus,* and made him out to be a devil.

The Dark Ages were full of fat rats and skinny cats. It was an utterly terrible time for cats, and not much better for people. The brilliant Greeks, basking in the sunshine of knowledge, were all but forgotten in the miasma of superstition that followed. People became terrified of shadows. The cat suffered; rats never had it so good. But because of the plague they caused, man, with unwavering allegiance from the cat, has kept the rodent population on the lam ever since.

Eventually, people once again came to accept the

PLINK

cat as a useful ally, and the cat began to prosper.

Now we come to our star attraction, the modern, up-to-date, ultra-sophisticated house cat, *felis domestica calculata*. There are twenty-seven million cats, more or less, according to the census taker. We don't know how he arrived at this figure, but rumor has it that he is now reposing in a rest home where he is being held incommunicado.

The point is there are an awful lot of cats.

The really great thing about cats is their endless variety. One can pick a cat to fit almost any kind of decor, color scheme, income, personality, mood, and so on. But under the fur, whatever color it may be, there still lies, essentially unchanged, one of the world's free souls.

As he has done through the ages, he is thinking . . . thinking. Let us turn now to a study of some of the things that might be occupying that brilliant little mind.

2
Cats and Their Family Life

In all good bookstores there are any number of books dealing with the care of cats. Some of these works are quite scholarly treatises, incredibly comprehensive, and others would simply cause any well-adjusted cat to snicker behind his whiskers. Cats for the most part are well adjusted, but few, if any, have ever learned to read. So when their time comes to have a family, they simply have it without the benefit of a Doctor Spock. To understand whether your cat is able to have a family is a matter of much study; and until you are absolutely certain what you have

in the way of a cat, I suggest you give it a name like Leslie, Albert, Victor, or some such which is readily converted to a feminine counterpart. For once you have named your cat William Lyon Phelps the Third, there is not much you can do about it, except find another name when your "male" cat becomes pregnant. Imagine how embarrassing this can be in front of your friends.

To have kittens, cats have to mate. This appears to be an undisputed fact. True, there are all sorts of rumors about storks. But we should generally put this kind of thing down for the folklore it is. It is perfectly absurd for storks, being birds, to voluntarily bring another cat into the world.

A logical explanation . . .

of the evolution

of a Tiger Cat . . .?

The mating of a cat follows simple, long-established procedures. The setting is usually a back fence, a moonlit night, and a house full of snoring humans. The female waits patiently for her suitors to arrive. Eventually they come. They climb the back fence and soon the night air is filled with the harmony of their singing. One of them, spoiling for a fight, chooses to sing off-key. This leads to a general free-for-all with much yeowling, punctuated by a steady stream of alarm clocks, shoes, flying saucers, and other assorted do-it-yourself missiles. Cats fight very hard for their true love, much like the heroes of the romantic novel, except that they fight with claws instead of swords. Eventually when the dust settles, along with the inner workings of various alarm clocks, there will be found one victorious male cat. As it ever was, to the victor belong the spoils. Note that the wooer of the fair lady is not selected by size of bank account, long and regal lineage, nor any other artificiality. He is selected for his strength, his intelligence, his courage. For this reason, there is always the chance, just as in any good romantic novel, for the low-born cat to win the paw of the beautiful female.

Now breeders, being of a less romantic turn of mind, do not like to take chances. For this reason they mate cats under controlled conditions. They choose from carefully selected blood lines with a definite goal in mind.

Some anti-catters get that way because they are snobs. They don't like to associate with beings who cannot produce pedigrees. Often they make mention of the fact that they are related to some important historical figure like the thirteenth cousin twice removed of Richard the Third, or the second cousin of George Washington's favorite drummer boy. Cats ignore this. In their infinite wisdom they know the only important heritage one can have is having a mother and father.

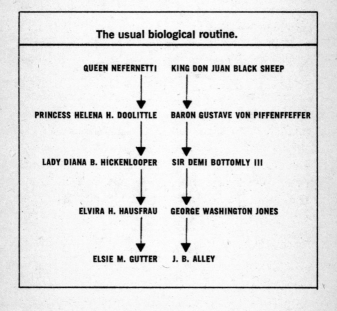

The usual biological routine.

QUEEN NEFERNETTI	KING DON JUAN BLACK SHEEP
↓	↓
PRINCESS HELENA H. DOOLITTLE	BARON GUSTAVE VON PIFFENFFEFFER
↓	↓
LADY DIANA B. HICKENLOOPER	SIR DEMI BOTTOMLY III
↓	↓
ELVIRA H. HAUSFRAU	GEORGE WASHINGTON JONES
↓	↓
ELSIE M. GUTTER	J. B. ALLEY

Among cats . . .

the course of True Love . . .

hardly ever . . .

runs smooth . . .

and . . .

they always . . .

live happily . . .

ever after . . .?

The male cat is not much as a father. He is like the happy Frenchman, a bachelor at heart. He wants to roam and be free of all responsibility for his family, and though the winning and wooing of his fair lady is rather tough on the hide, he would not have any other life but his own. Soon he is off into the world looking for new conquests. He recalls past glories and picaresque adventures. For instance, the time he was cornered in the church belfry not unlike poor Quasimodo, when the apprentice bellringer decided to get in some practice.

No matter where we are . . .

sooner or later . . .

we will find . . .

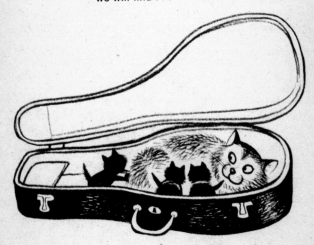

that female cats are Wonderful Mothers.

Like mothers everywhere, the cat has her work cut out for her. She must train her offspring in almost all phases of activity. This is fortunate, because cats simply refuse to learn from humans.

Basic training consists of teaching the kittens how to win over the master by curling up in his lap, purring, and looking lovingly at him. This is essential, because it makes it very hard for the master to give them away. Also on the agenda is how to chase a stuffed mouse, bits of paper, balls of yarn, and other ridiculous objects to further please the master. Other fundamentals include how to look innocent when caught eating on top of the dining room table, and how to sharpen the claws on the sofa, which shortly takes on the look of a very badly designed sheep dog.

Yes, mother has her work cut out for her. In all things she is a model mother, bathing her young when they need it and even when they don't need it, picking them up when they fall, carrying them to and fro, always ready to answer their slightest miaow, and perfectly willing, if necessary in protecting her offspring, to scratch your eyes out.

As they grow older, their education . . .

in cat ways . . .

. . . is supervised and directed.

She always shows her pupils . . .

the very worst place to bring their trophies . . .

. . . and where they should be most appreciated . . .

. . . but seldom are.

Mother's idea of what she considers to be sensible training for her kittens may differ widely from the human conception of sensible training. Mother cats sometimes don't appreciate this fact, and are continually frustrated by bigger and uglier humans. Is it any wonder that mother simply gives the whole business up as a bad job?

The one disadvantage of having cats (female, un-fixed) is that rarely do they contrive to have one kitten at a time. They have a squad at a time, some-times enough for a basketball team with a spare cen-ter and forward. When they all start to dribble bits of paper about the house, or reconnoiter every single dark corner, the owner of said house begins to feel that he is beset by a platoon of fast-moving little furry commandos.

If the demolition really gets out of hand, the in-evitable must come. The kittens simply have to be found new homes to take over. This is a project in itself, and takes every bit of the skill any ingenuity man has acquired over the past million-give-or-take-a-few-thousand years. It requires the cunning of a chess master, the planning of a field marshal, the adroitness and polish of a premier of France, or, fail-ing these, the sheer, unmitigated gall of your door-to-door salesman.

Sometimes just plain "Influence" takes care of the
problem of getting kittens suitably placed.

Kittens are wonderfully co-operative, and with the help of another animal, can do a fine job of selling themselves.

Many are the tricks used to find the kittens a new home.

In any event, you may not have to pick out a cat. He may pick you out.

3

So Now You Own
a Cat?

By one of the various methods mentioned in our
previous chapter, you have come to be the owner of
a kitten. Actually this is not quite true. Let us say
that you have chosen to share your domicile with a
kitten. Now there are certain important rules to observe. First, before welcoming a kitten into your
home, it is suggested that you gather as much information about your house guest as possible.

There is a case history of a man who procured one kitten, unknown gender, unknown ancestry. The kitten started to grow. At the end of six weeks it weighed six pounds. At the end of twelve weeks, the cat had grown so large that the owner was forced to make a token payment of a fish before he entered the front door. The cat was actually running the house like a set of toll stations. Our man began to wonder seriously if he had a domesticated house cat (which it wasn't), slowly coming to the conclusion, after some tardy research, that his cat must be a bob cat (which it was). The owner was forced to move out of the house shortly after the bob cat chewed through the legs of the bedstead and dropped the master on the floor. Of course this is a wondrous tale to be able to tell your grandchildren and you may consider the effort worth it. At the very least, it will enliven your cocktail conversation and you might get the little fellow's picture in the newspaper. However, you must keep a full refrigerator and purchase some good iron underwear when engaged in this type of status seeking.

For some cats, prompt feeding is desirable.

HERE
KITTY
KITTY

Cats are finicky eaters. If they do not like what you are feeding them, they will simply refuse it. They won't bark at you, but will simply look at the meal with devastating scorn, point their tail straight up in the air, and go off to sleep in some corner, scowling darkly the while. Cats with a touch of the epicure in them do this at least once a week to prevent the quality of the food from deteriorating. It does keep one on one's toes, and often the cat is so successful at this occupation that he can make people spend more time planning *his* meals than planning their own. Very clever of the cat.

Quite often cats feel they are our equals, if not our superiors. For this reason the idea of eating from a bowl which is placed on a newspaper on the kitchen floor, while we are eating at a table from a plate, is not entirely to a cat's liking. Actually this status differentiation between cats and people is most offensive to the general run of cats, and actually intolerable to a few ultra-sophisticated cats. The result is that your cat will spend a considerable amount of time trying, not only to find out what you are eating, but how he can wheedle some of it for himself. The ready cure for this is to have a bowl of onion soup. When the cat looks at you as if you had poisoned his food, permit him to jump up on the table and sample the soup. To save face he will be forced to at least sniff it very carefully, after which he may regard the whole business as a dirty trick and plan his revenge accordingly. However, there is a good chance that you may get to have your soup, though slightly used, in peace.

Humans sleep. Cats sleep also, but for the most part, cats take cat naps. Let us say that it is late at night. The master of the house turns the lights on in the kitchen. He notices that the cat is asleep. The owner opens the refrigerator and makes a left-handed, up-to-the-elbows grab for a chicken leg located toward the rear of one of the top shelves. In so doing he dislodges something potentially slippery, say a banana. As the master of the house turns around, he slips on the banana, lets the chicken leg go where it will, and hits the floor with a bone-shattering crash. If and when he gets up, he notices the cat is still sleeping and the chicken leg cannot be found. Strange.

58

Often you will find . . .

that your . . .

hat will fit . . .

your cat better than you.

Actually the cat woke up when the refrigerator door opened, fell asleep, woke up again when the master fell, calculated with mathematical precision that he would not be crushed, and woke up the third time to catch a glimpse of a chicken leg sailing through the air which he deftly fielded and back-handed far under the refrigerator for future reference.

Cats are quite particular about where they sleep. They are not likely to sleep in the basket which has been purchased specifically for this purpose. True, the basket may have been designed with the most careful consideration in mind, orthopedically constructed to prevent curvature of the spine, soft to ensure a dreamless sleep, and all that. But cats do not like to sleep in out-of-the-way places because they have to drag themselves from their sleeping quarters all the way to some place where something is likely to happen. This is the only way they can satisfy their sense of curiosity. For this reason, they will sleep nearly anywhere, if there is the possibility of something happening. If you should find your cat asleep on the edge of a bathtub, and he wakes up when you enter, do not advance a step farther. The chances are that he simply wants to see what will happen when you step on that cake of soap in the middle of the floor.

Victorian frills have their uses.

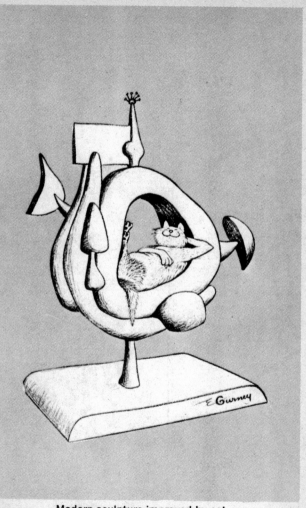

Modern sculpture improved by cat.

4
Care and Grooming
of Cats

The terror of a man who
thinks he is going bald.

Cats, for the most part, take quite good care of themselves. However, there are a few things which a cat requires for his continuing good health and peace of mind.

Like people, cats benefit from a spot of physical activity to make their whiskers stand out properly, to ensure a good coat, and to make it easier for them to get up on the dining room table. Cats used to get this exercise a long time ago by catching mice and other prey. But a few of your modern, ultra-sophisticated, spoiled-rotten type cats might not recognize a mouse if you dangled one in front of their noses.

So we are faced with the problem of providing exercise for our cats in other ways. Most people put the cat outside in the hope that he will go dashing around and climb a few trees. Rarely effective. Instead the cat will probably beat it around the house to the front door and proceed to scratch his way in. This is exercise of a sort, but it is only worth the candle if you happen to enjoy refinishing woodwork.

However a cat *will* climb trees from time to time, and if he happens to be out of practice, this can be a problem. There is an old rumor that what goes up must of necessity be dragged down. This has never been translated into cat language with sufficient clarity. Cats have a way of rewriting the rules. They have to be dragged down from the tops of trees with such a monotonous regularity that some people come to be quite expert at rescuing cats. I witnessed a masterful display of technique just the other day and have sketched it for this chapter.

From here the view is mighty fine . . .

. . . it sends a shiver up my spine.

There are a good many dog salons throughout the world. You can take a dog to any of the better ones and get his nails manicured, his hair clipped, his hide bathed, his whiskers trimmed, his feet booted, his back coated, and his tail bobbed, to list just the routine services available. And I am sure that some nut will psychoanalyze your silly pooch, assuming you can withstand the fee. I have it on good authority that a book with the rather fetching title *How to Live with a Neurotic Dog* has been published with astonishing success here and abroad.

It is a pity no one has provided the same range of services for cats. There must be a profit to be realized from running cat salons in which the same general principles, gleaned over the centuries from the care and grooming of dogs, could be readily applied. Needless to say, the insurance rates would have to go up for those engaged in such practices. Cats simply won't have any of these procedures, and are admirably equipped to make the point.

Dogs often tangle with skunks. It is suspected that these encounters give humans the idea that all domesticated animals need baths from time to time. Cats, however, being the sophisticated animals they are, wouldn't be caught dead within three hundred yards of a skunk. Is it possible to come to the conclusion that cats do not need baths? Further, consider the cat's tongue. How admirably the cat's tongue is designed to enable him to bathe himself. Also, there is the matter of the cat's status. No self-respecting cat would dream of being introduced to another cat with a single hair out of place. Why, it would be like finding the President with holes in his dungarees.

In conclusion, if you should recklessly decide to give your cat a bath, change your mind and don't. If you still insist on being hard-headed about the whole affair, get some soap designed to do the job, draw a tub of water brought carefully up to cat-body temperature, a towel or two, iodine, sutures, gauze (a bottle of brandy wouldn't be amiss), and a pair of chain-mail gauntlets. You might also notify your next of kin if you are the type that really plans ahead.

Disaster comes in small bottles.

Fleas are good underwater swimmers.

Half drowned, but still standing.

Artificial Respiration.

Another advertising claim . . .

. . . comes to naught.

First, you catch your cat and put him in the tub. Then you lather up the cat, if you are still able to, followed by a rinse, if the cat is still able to.

Now you dry the cat ever so carefully to prevent any blood from dripping on the clean fur. After this you can let the cat go and you could have a tot of that brandy. The cat will immediately find a good place to roll where he can get himself dirty from stem to stern, after which he will lick himself clean. This really gets a cat's tongue very tired, and many won't purr for months.

Her own mother wouldn't know her.

Cats are similarly neat about their claws, which they clean by scratching. Some people are under the impression that almost anything will serve this purpose. Nothing could be further from the truth. Any cat worth his tuna would instantly be sent to Coventry by his fellows if he sharpened his claws on anything less than the very best. Therefore, at the top of the list as recommended scratching mediums come linen, family portrait, tapestries, batik, satins, Dior originals, and the like. Down at the very bottom of the list are logs, trees, and those silly scratching posts. If you are worried about your cat turning your house into a shambles, be at ease. He will only do it a stick or two of furniture at a time. Trimming a cat's claws is all right provided he does not have to defend himself from tall dogs. While cats resent this treatment, they are bound to gain new respect for people; and may even come to the conclusion that some are really quite smart after all.

Sometimes cats require more important medication. They may require pills just as people do. As with the bath, however, we have problems. The usual approach is the jam-it-down-his-throat-before-he-bites-you technique. In no circumstances should you try this method on a cat without prior experience unless you have the uncanny ability of growing new fingers. Before you proceed, a few trial runs on a six-year-old child may prove invaluable training for you.

The soft sell approach . . .

is always . . .

HOMP
OMP

successful . . .

...?

Any cat . . .

who fights this hard . . .

hardly needs . . .

to take . . .

. . . vitamins.

The only way . . .

to play the game . . .

is to cheat.

A Final Reminder: It has been observed that some of to-day's vitamin pills are fairly potent. In rare cases your doctor may decide to adjust the dosage.

5
Cat Lovers and
Cat Haters

A Phobia In Action.

A recent survey revealed that out of every 250 people, 216 are cat lovers, 54 are cat haters, and the rest are not voting this year. From these results we can see why surveys shouldn't be taken too seriously.

The people who hate cats form quite an interesting group. I have created a little rogues' gallery of cat haters so that you will be able to pick out their counterparts from among your friends (if you do not have a cat to do this for you).

The most unusual type of cat hater is the person who hates them because he is terrified of them. They have a long name for this, but for the life of me I can't remember it. However, it is something or other ending in phobia. I don't pretend to know how one catches this phobia, nor even if it is contagious, nor what will get rid of it.

There is also a group of people whose hobbies contrast rather violently with those of the cat. These people are only anti-catters part of the time, but they make up for this part-time occupation by the vigor with which they pursue it.

Mice are also anti-catters, and of course for the best reason. The only time they get the better of the cat is in cartoons, or other comic situations, including any dreaming they may do.

Ignatz, a famous cat hater, accomplishes the impossible.

© King Features. All rights reserved.

Some people are anti-catters for reasons of health. The majority are simply allergic to cats. They may not even know a cat is around until their radarlike noses inform them of the fact. Too bad they aren't allergic to submarines or pickpockets. The remainder of this group who believe cats can influence health live for the most part in lion, tiger, or leopard country. They believe life can be considerably shortened by the presence of a very large, mean, and hungry beast. A few rabid anti-catters go so far as to say that hungry or not, the lion, tiger, leopard, or whatnot will eat you on general principles or just to keep his hand in.

As a . . .

matter . . .

of fact . . .

they may not . . .

even be aware . . .

that . . .

AHHHH

. . . a cat is around until they start sneezing!

CHEW

A Typical Cat Hater.

Dictators, who are simply do-it-yourself kings of questionable ancestry and unspeakable table manners, don't, as a rule, like cats. At bottom, it is just that dictators find the independent air in the cat quite intolerable. Freedom is the very last thing a dictator wants to have on his mind. This has led some scholars, cartoonists, foreign correspondents, etc., to the conclusion that dictators are related to certain rodents that don't like cats either. Thus dictators don't like cats because cats don't like them.

Cat Si . . . Mussolini No.

Napoleon had his Waterloo. . . . He also had his rats.

A Typical Cats-Come-First-People-Come-Second Cat Lover...

Now, happily, we come to the cat lover. He will have one cat on tap at all times, and maybe more. However, the genuine cats-come-first-people-come-second type of cat lover will tell you that you don't even get into the club unless you have at least four. Now you may say four cats are all right; but four cats means four very fertile cats with full permission to let nature take its course. Cat lovers can readily be identified without any assistance from us. No matter what they wear, their clothes always look old and well used. Their sheets look like bath towels, and their bath towels look like a collection of knitting mistakes.

Mark Twain . . .

Lincoln and Cat on Independence.

. . . and to my cat, one million tax-free dollars.

Undoubtedly the most unusual cat lover is the individual who, upon deciding he can't stand his relatives and what the hell he can't take it with him, chooses to leave everything to his cat, Tobermory. This poses an interesting problem; for cats, intelligence notwithstanding, do not have the necessary equipment to endorse the numerous checks involved. True, they can be admirably employed in canceling their checks with their teeth. For this reason cats have to have trustees down at the bank, which is about the only time that people really get to know exactly what it is like to be employed by a cat.

Crib Sheet

The purpose of this sheet is to help you to cheat without actually winning. Look at the questions on the next page, then study the hints below.

Hint to Question One: Alexander the Great threw a spear over his best friend's head and missed. This made Alexander very sad. But it is not known which he regretted the more, the killing of his friend or his bad aim.

Hint to Question Two: Unlike Alexander, Caesar was killed by his best friend. Caesar wrote a very dull set of chronicles telling how he subjugated his enemies. Latin students have been punished ever since.

Hint to Question Three: Mussolini had a very stiff neck which prevented him from seeing the ground. This deficiency eventually tripped him up.

Hint to Question Four: Napoleon was a frustrated man who thought power could take the place of greatness. He marched an army underground and a navy underwater. Now he lies under a huge stone lid to prevent him from escaping again.

Hint to Question Five: Silly is a good answer to this question. Sick is another good answer too.

Hint to Question Six: It depends on the size of the cats, but mention any goodly amount.

Hint to Question Seven: How high do you keep your food?

Cat Lovers

Petrarch
Cardinal Wolsey
Montaigne
Victor Hugo
Samuel Johnson
Walter Scott
Matthew Arnold
Baudelaire
Lincoln
Washington
Schweitzer

Cat Haters

Alexander the Great
Julius Caesar
Napoleon
Mussolini

Question One: Who would you like to have as your best friend? Alexander the Great or George Washington?

Question Two: Who would you prefer to lose a war to? Julius Caesar or Lincoln?

Question Three: Who would you trust on a safari in Africa? Mussolini or Albert Schweitzer?

Question Four: With whom would you like to take a long walk? Napoleon or Samuel Johnson?

Question Five: Is it silly or smart to have forty cats?

Question Six: How much would forty cats eat in one week?

Question Seven: How high can a cat jump?

Answers

1. George Washington. Some of George Washington's detractors point out that he did a very stupid thing; he chopped down a cherry tree. If that is the only stupid thing he did, he was a very great man indeed.

2. Lincoln. Though both came from humble origins and both had assassins, Lincoln was the greater magician. He was an ugly man, and yet most free men think he was quite beautiful. This is a trick which we could all learn.

3. Schweitzer. He spent his life in trying to keep people above the ground. Mussolini put a good many people in it past their ears.

4. Johnson. Walking with a man who could talk so well would always be a pleasure and might even have made the Russian hike passable, if not feasible.

5. Silly. Obviously that old saw, "The more the merrier," should be taken with a grain of salt.

6. I don't know, but start out with one cow, or one third of a small hippopotamus, or one eighth of an elephant, or one billion sixty-three caviar eggs.

7. This depends on how high up in a tree he is.

How to Score Yourself: Give yourself 14.28571428-571428571 for each correct answer.

6
Cats and Other Animals

When you first bring a cat into the house, and you have other household pets, you can expect a certain amount of trouble during the adjustment period. For instance, if you have birds, or fish, you can expect your cat to develop a very short focal point of interest to which he will devote a large number of his waking hours. Getting a canary out of a cage, or a fish out of an aquarium, becomes an intellectual challenge for a cat; and it will become an intellectual challenge for you to prevent this from happening. You may find your cat sleeping patiently on a sofa near the bird cage. Don't be fooled by this. He is merely studying with great care how he can manage the latch, open the door, and bag the canary as quietly as possible. He is luckier with fish because fish don't make any noise, and you may find your cat enticing your prize guppy to the top of the tank with a carefully dangled paw, one claw barely dipping into the water. By wiggling this bit of a claw around like a trout fly, he leads the guppy to believe this is food and rise to it, with the usual results.

Generally speaking, your dog and cat will not hit it off at all well in the beginning. Dogs instinctively realize that cats are smarter than they are, so they resent the intrusion of a cat upon the household. The dog doesn't exactly look at the cat as if he were dinner on the hoof, but it is very hard to tell this as your dog goes streaking after your cat. Given a reasonable chance, your cat will simply avoid being caught. The only reason the cat runs away from the dog in the first place instead of clawing his eyes out, is that your cat instinctively knows your dog thinks he is king of the castle, which is exactly what the cat wants him to think.

Cats and people love birds . . . for different reasons.

The dog will continue to chase the cat until such time as the cat decides the dog is beginning to lose his judgment. This the cat can do by studying the condition of the dog's eyes. But to make absolutely certain, the cat will casually walk close to the dog to see what happens. The dog will slowly rise to his feet and weakly chase the cat about. He is like a man half-asleep behind the wheel. His steering lacks the fine coordination required to negotiate the turns around the furniture. Knowing the dog is ready, the cat will dash between your legs while you are holding something breakable. The dog will try to follow, but won't fit. Crash goes the bric-a-brac and out goes the dog. As the canine culprit looks forlornly through the window, he will see you-know-who staring at him with a silly little smile playing about his whiskers.

The second phase of training begins at this point. This consists of your cat's enlisting the help of a bigger, surlier dog than yours. The cat may do this by showing said bigger, surlier dog your dog's food dish. If your dog objects to these procedures, he is going to have a very rough time of it, indeed. However, should you own the larger, surlier dog, your cat will merely observe where he hides his bones and carefully broadcast the news to the general neighborhood. An army of dogs will at once advance, and your dog will rush forth to combat this invasion. However, while he is busy chasing one off, another interloper will be busy digging up your petunias. Your dog will eventually get hysterical over these events, but he will not have a single growl left in him by the time the last bone is moved from your yard to parts unknown.

By this time your dog is willing to concede victory to the cat. The cat, realizing this, will curl up to your dog and watch him. Your dog will be too tired to object, and will permit this familiarity which he wouldn't have tolerated a week or so earlier. Now right here you have the beginning of the most dangerous kind of combination, a really good cat-and-dog team. You may not realize how many opportunities offer themselves to a really top-notch cat-and-dog combination. Let us say that you have finished dinner and left a good bit of the roast on the kitchen table. Now the dog cannot get up on the table, but the cat can. But the cat cannot carry the roast away, whereas the dog can. Obviously, one can see what well-coordinated teamwork can accomplish here. But what you may not see is how far this teamwork may

The Cat's Motto: Help stamp out faithful, trustworthy, and devoted dogs.

A friend . . .

in need . . .

is a . . .

friend indeed.

be carried out in this mundane circumstance. As you may have suspected, the cat will hop up on the table and bulldoze the roast off the table into the dog's mouth. Dog will then carry it outside where they will both proceed to stuff themselves. But what is actually involved is far more sophisticated and calculated, a study in masterly preparation and faultless execution. It merits our attention. Let's run through it quickly.

First, dog sniffs the roast. Cat takes a triangulated compass reading on dog's nose to determine the exact location of the roast on the table so that he won't end up in the middle of the mashed potatoes when he jumps. Second, cat climbs up on dog's back to make the leap as short as possible in the event that the table is wobbly. Cat then hops onto the table and pushes the roast off the table, Note, he doesn't push it onto the floor where it might go splat—too much noise. He pushes it into dog's mouth, so that you won't hear a thing. Cat then licks the table clean to remove any evidence, and also licks the floor in case dog has been a trifle clumsy, though the cat-educated dog rarely makes such a mistake. The remaining problem is how to get the repast out of the house where it may be enjoyed at leisure without interference. The simplest method is for cat to distract your attention. He might streak through the house toward something breakable. Meanwhile, during this moment of distraction, dog and roast do a fast fade. Curtain.

Teamwork makes the impossible simple.

Some cats are such artful fagins that they are never caught, managing to get into anything edible without the slightest trace of suspicion falling on them. This goes to show you that the old saw about man being a dog's best friend is not always correct. Ask any cat-indoctrinated dog and he will tell you that his best friend is a cat. Ask me. Some of my best friends are cats.

7

Cat Quirks

There is an old wives' tale that a cat brushing his paw past the tip of his ear is a forecast of rain. No one believes this harmless superstition any more . . . which is a pity.

This is a typical cat quirk. Yes, cats have quirks just as people do, only the quirks which cats have are perhaps more sensible. A typical cat quirk is that they can purr. We don't pretend to know exactly what kind of a mechanism goes into the making of a purr, or how to wind it up once it runs down. However, this much is known: There are a wide variety of purrs which range from the almost inaudible to the kind which can be felt through the floor. Loud purring might possibly set up sympathetic vibrations in a building and send it crashing to the ground. For these reasons, as well as others too numerous to mention, lions make very poor household pets.

A typical cat quirk is a well-developed sense of curiosity. Curiosity is also a quirk of humans. However, cats are admirably designed to be curious. They have excellent hearing (except when you call them into the house). Their soft pads allow them to walk about softly with a minimum amount of disturbance (except when you are trying to sleep). Thus cats can sneak up on all kinds of creatures without being observed. This allows cats to see things as they are, a fact which makes them wonderful naturalists. As naturalists, we humans have a rough time of it because of our big feet. Sooner or later, when we are sneaking up on some shy woodland creature, we are bound to step on a stick which gives the whole show away. As if this were not enough, naturalists get lost; and they can't find their way around in the dark without a flashlight. Cats, on the other hand, have supersensitive eyes for seeing in the dark, and, even when they cannot see, whiskers that warn them of the presence of objects over which we stumble helplessly, if not break our necks. Some researchers have theorized that cats use their whiskers as a very elaborate compass system, taking a series of bearings on the ends of these same whiskers to find their way home. (This might explain the occasional wall-eyed cat we see, by the way.) This must be reasonable, for cats rarely get lost when they go larking in the woods. In fairness to our cats, meticulous care of these whiskers should be one of our prime considerations. They are the keenest barometer of his well-being.

The perkiness, droop, crinkle of his whiskers are symptoms of his physical and mental health. When his whiskers are gracefully curled, he will be at his fittest, as well as his sanest.

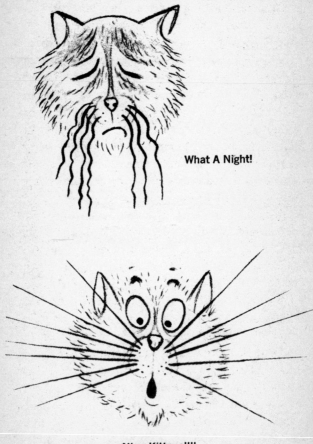

What A Night!

Nine Kittens!!!!

Smile when you call me that.

The Grand Exit

Foe .

Friend Or Foe?

127

Well, I'm waiting.

Dearie, I know where you can go,
but I can't tell you how to get there.

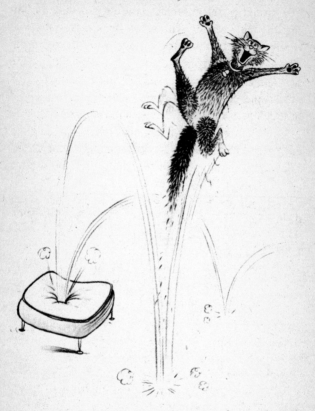

The term "Crazy Cat" is just a description of a cat letting herself go.

Another problem which naturalists have is signaling to one another without making any unnatural noises. Some of these tricks have been learned from Tarzan films or from the Indians and might include hooting like an owl, screeching like a loon (which may come naturally to some people), or, in lieu of bird call proficiency, clicking rocks together.

Cats, on the other hand, are adept at signaling each other with their tails, and mothers spend a considerable amount of time teaching their kittens this sign language. This is quite a task because of the dialects involved. It has even been said that a cat from the North cannot possibly understand a cat from the South. However, after considerable study I feel that cats have adopted a tail language much like Esperanto which, with sufficient effort, can be understood the world over.

The most unusual quirk a cat can develop is introduced by an herb commonly known as catnip.

After being exposed to catnip, cats, in the main, go quietly berserk until they are completely exhausted. I would be most remiss if I didn't make the point here that catnip, like heroin, pistachio nuts, gin, crossword puzzles, cigars, etc., can be habit forming. Indeed, many an otherwise splendid animal has lost everything once this habit got the better of him. The answer, as we all know, is to get him interested in your local chapter of Catnippers Anonymous, *providing he has the insight to take that first step.*

130

8
Some Very Famous Calculating Cats

Milton said fame was the last disease of noble minds. Cats must have come to this conclusion a long time ago, for they do not seem to be much concerned with becoming famous. The reason they are not interested in becoming famous is simply that they cannot eat fame, and fame is not a cozy home, nor the fifty or sixty sleeping places to which a normal cat is accustomed. Milton notwithstanding, there are some famous cats. So we must doff our hats and enter those reverent halls where the great cats of the past are honored, and pussy-foot our way around in silence.

First, we come to Dick Whittington's cat. It appears that a certain merchant expressed a desire that his servants invest their money in some foreign venture. Foreign trade, being what it was in those days before the common market, was a risky business, so Dick Whittington chose to donate a cat to the project. In one of the countries the merchant visited, there were hoards of four-footed, bona-fide rats. Dick's cat finished them all, one by one. A reward was paid for the service, not to the cat but to Dick, who eventually became Lord Mayor of London, a position he acquired with the aid of a helping paw.

A mathematician named Lewis Carroll wrote an adventure about a little girl named Alice who met, among other strange beings, a Cheshire cat lying on the limb of a tree. This cat had the oddest quirk of all. He could disappear tail first, leaving only his grin behind. This made Alice exclaim that she had seen a cat without a grin, but never a grin without a cat. This unique trick happily died with its perpetrator's disappearance. The Cheshire cat's real claim to fame, however, is that he was the first cat to admit quite cheerfully that he was mad.

135

PUSS IN BOOTS, BY CHARLES PERRAULT

A miller left his youngest son a very clever cat who decided quite simply to make the miller's son rich. This he did diplomatically by relying on the gullibility of a king. Puss needed a castle for his master to convince the king that the miller's son was indeed a wealthy prince. Finding that a local ogre owned quite a nice castle, he sweet-talked the ogre into performing certain feats of magic. Willing to show off in front of his captive audience, the ogre made the mistake of converting himself into a mouse on request and *he* became the captive audience. The cat found the ogre-mouse wasn't very toothsome, but ate him anyway. Such gullibility in ogres has made them all but extinct in modern times.

© King Features. All rights reserved.

Krazy Kat, a particular pet of George Herriman and King Features, never made anyone rich. He was simply one of those honest, not overly bright cats who tried to do the right thing. He was continually thwarted in these efforts by a dishonest, thieving mouse, Ignatz. Krazy's particular nemesis usually won the first round, then ended up being hauled off to jail by Offissa Pupp. Ignatz had a record as long as your arm but always seemed able to make bail in order to be ready for the next day's escapades.

Richard the Lion Hearted was a great warrior who had trouble with a certain person named Saladin over a piece of property called Jerusalem. Richard left both the lion and the trouble as a legacy to the world. On the whole the British have done pretty well for themselves. Some people claim that is because they are, like the lion, beef-eaters. Some others, however, claim the British Empire was founded by people who didn't like the weather back home.

* THE PRINCETON TIGER

The Princeton Tiger is a very sociable fellow. It is suspected that he was adopted as a mascot simply because he was the only creature big enough to beat a certain bulldog known as Handsome Dan. However, this has not always been the case, as any good Yale man will tell you, given the slightest opportunity. In any event, any similarity between the Princeton Tiger usually found around Fifth Avenue and Forty-third Street and those found in the jungle is purely coincidental.

Your cat may become famous, too. However, it is doubtful that he will be able to make you very rich because of the taxes. So do not expect your cat to be a tangible asset. His tendency is to drift into the other side of the ledger. Also there is a possibility that you will find your cat insufferable, once he is famous. If you think this might be the case, place him on a pedestal in front of a mirror. Watch his response and act accordingly.

As you can see, the ultra-sophisticated, modern, up-to-date domesticated cat has a pretty good life. His great, great, great grandfather probably thinks he is a playboy.